G000114645

Some Unease and Angels

Elaine Feinstein

Some Unease and Angels SELECTED POEMS

Hutchinson of London

Hutchinson & Co (Publishers) Ltd
3 Fitzroy Square, London W1P 6JD

London Melbourne Sydney Auckland
Wellington Johannesburg and agencies
throughout the world

First published in this collection 1977
© in this collection
Elaine Feinstein 1977

Set in IBM Theme by D.P.Media Limited
Hitchin, Herts.

Printed in Great Britain by
The Anchor Press Ltd, and bound by
Wm Brendon & Son Ltd, both of
Tiptree, Essex

ISBN 0 09 129851 2

For Emma

Contents

Three translations from the Russian of Marina Tsvetayeva
(literal versions made by Angela Livingstone)

Homage to Marina Tsvetayeva by three Russian poets

Father

The wood trade in his hands
at sixtyone back at the sawbench,
my stubborn father sands and planes
birchwood for kitchen chairs.

All my childhood he was a rich man
unguarded purchaser
of salmon trout, off-season strawberries
and spring in Switzerland.

Bully to prudish aunts
whose niggard habits taught them to assess
honest advantage, without rhetoric:
his belly laughter overbore their tutting.

Still boss of his own shop
he labours in the chippings without grudge
loading the heavy tables,
shabby and powerful as an old bus.

Calliope in the labour ward

she who has no love for women
married and housekeeping

now the bird notes begin
in the blood in the June morning
look how these ladies are
as little squeamish as
men in a great war

have come into their bodies
as their brain dwindles to
the silver circle on
eyelids under sun
and time opens
pain in the shallows to wave up and over them

grunting in gas and air
they sail to a
darkness without self
where no will reaches

in that abandon less
than human
give birth
bleak as a goddess

Mother love

You eat me, your
nights eat me
Once you took
haemoglobin and bone
out of my blood

Now my head
sleeps forward on my neck
holding you

In the morning my
skin shines hot
and you are happy
banging your fat hands

I kiss your
soft feet mindless:
delicately

your shit slides out
yellow and
smelling of curd cheese.

Annie

Old aunt your
ginger hair grey
eyes are ashes

scattered: to
forget them freely
I think of you

living up North
Matron of a
hospital. You

talked with a cigarette
smoking your nose
a spinster underneath

your clothes fastidious
lilac knickers lace
over your corset a

bosom like a bolster.
Back from Sark
you were as

clean as a
sea bird in your
lonely virtue

Now with your Will, I
read you forgive us
all   give us

(we squanderers)
what you put by
living within your pension

and how shall I
    thank you where
your lost grey sand

is shaken into
the Northern air

Aubade for a scientist

To see your sadness
your lonely stupor
downstairs in a chair
asleep, your glasses
up in your hair,
your face unused

You are flying
(books at your feet and
typescript in your hand)
over the maple, the
horse chestnut: how
shall I wake you

to the tether of
these dimensions?
Symbols lie on
the paper: will you
look through their lines
and hope for crevices
open to strange light?

Song of Power

For the baiting
children in my
son's school class who
say I am a witch:
black is the
mirror you give me

drawn inward at siege
sightless, mumbling:
criminal, to bear three
children like fruit
cannot be guarded
against enemies.

Should I have lived sterile?
The word returns me.
If any supernatural power
my strangeness earns me
I now invoke, for
all Gods are

anarchic even the Jews'
outside his own laws, with
his old name
confirms me, and I
call out for the
strange ones with wild hair

all the earth over to
make their own coherence
a fire their children
may learn to bear at last
and not burn in.

At seven a son

In cold weather on a
garden swing, his legs
in wellingtons rising over
the winter rose trees

he sits serenely
smiling like a Thai
his coat open, his gloves
sewn to the flapping sleeves

his thin knees working
with his arms
folded about the
metal struts

as he flies up
(his hair like long
black leaves) he
lies back freely

astonished in
sunshine as serious
as a stranger he is
a bird in his own thought.

Morning car rides

Shall I fear for you as the
farmer's children answer
the bright malice of your
logic? You are too
thin for these gestures

but your talent is not grave:
you are impudent as a
water hopper — and about
the bluntness of cruelty
need no teaching.

Daily whenever the car
pauses, meeting your eye
I puzzle at the black
disc flickering in
the blue of your eye shell

Adam

Once or twice your nightmare
woke us: your wet hair
smelling like a donkey
thin arms out you screamed
in a dream we never reached you through.

But last night sober you
woke up explaining how
the curtain jerks across
another Adam face screwed up,
breaks through the glass to get you

And 'brains are funny' you say
as setting things right
we talk today. But still go on
avoiding the eye of
windows even in daylight

A Dream of Spinsterhood

The wish for an unthinking reckless solitude — Franz Kafka

All that Sunday
for a beginning deserts
of space
a bright self
moving single as a blade

or cruising
bodiless as a ghost
through London streets
an eye   invisible
in noise and light

But when last night
dreaming with a dry mouth
I was 25
again   alone
obsessed with sex

I cried out
caught in a
Sunday tight
as a box
and woke up weeping

to touch you in relief:
over us
leaves moved on the
ceiling gentle as
water on the roof
of a stone bridge.

Politics

Later the cleaners come
cigarettes pinched in their lips
as they lean gossiping

and they are gristle and bone
innocent elbows
scrubbing out urinals
with silent eyes dreaming

washing the cupboards
watching the time to be done

and the baize door is open
the torturers
are outside in the sun

Against Winter

His kiss a bristling
beard in my ear, at 83:
'aren't you afraid of
dying? I asked him (on his knee).
who shall excel   his shrug for answer?

and yet was it long after,
senile, he lived in our front room,
once I had to
hold a potty out for him, his
penis was pink and clean as a child

and what he remembered of
Odessa and the Europe he walked through
was gone like the language I
never learned to speak, that
gave him resistance,

and his own sense of
favour: (failed
rabbi, carpenter,
farmer in
Montreal)

and now I think
how the smell of
peppermint in his yellow
handkerchieves and the
snuff marks under his nose

were another part of it:
his sloven grace
(stronger than abstinence) that
was the source of his
undisciplined stamina.

Anniversary

Suppose I took out a slender ketch from
under the spokes of Palace pier tonight to
catch a sea going fish for you

or dressed in antique goggles and wings and
flew down through sycamore leaves into the park

or luminescent through some planetary strike
put one delicate flamingo leg over the sill of your lab

Could I surprise you?   or would you insist on
keeping a pattern to link every transfiguration?

Listen, I shall have to whisper it
into your heart directly: we are all
supernatural / every day
we rise new creatures / cannot be predicted

The Magic Apple Tree

Sealed in rainlight one
November sleepwalking afternoon streets
I remembered Samuel Palmer's garden
Waterhouse in Shoreham, and at once
I knew: that the chill of wet
brown streets was no more literal
than the yellow he laid there against
his unnatural blue   because
together they worked upon me like
an icon   infantine

he called his vision / so it was
with the early makers of icons, who
worked humbly, choosing wood without resin.
They stilled their spirits before using the gold
and while the brightness held under the kvass
their colours too induced
the peculiar joy of abandoning restlessness

and now in streets where only white
mac or car metal catches the falling
light, if we sing of
the red and the blue and the texture of goat hair,
there is no deceit in our prophecy:
for even now our brackish waters can
be sweetened by a strange tree.

Moon

At first it seems as if the
    moon governs the fen, in the waters of
many estuaries, it is felt
    even beneath the fields, in the salt mud,
and it sits in August red on
    the long flowing extensions of land into sea.

Moon, loveless and lifeless, you
    bear upon the breeding about here
uneasily; long ago crossers of
    cold seas were the very last
invasion of this region, and
    since, whole villages have fallen into
that absolute purity of race: which is incest.

And so, old clinker, still
    circling our skies, I am
your enemy: I want by some transition
    to bring in strange black
people of the sun, among
    your good and graceless villagers,
not to do harm, only to
    have your own people remember certain
ancient songs without alarm.

I know the tyranny of landscape
    is strong, and the moon
remains entirely calm at my voice, however
    I have some disreputable allies
which even now enter the tied cottages
    by hidden electric cable.

(Yes I distrust them).   Nevertheless
   true singers will complete the violation
of this area: and when they come, they
   will find your own East Anglian children
already dancing. To an alien drum.

In the question of survival

You are the white
birth tree your thought
subtle and silver as
the morning air moving in
delicate leaves

and not to traduce your
sadness: it lights
your low voice so that
sane and sequent creatures
blunder grossly in the breath
of your quiet presence

and you are a minister of grace, a
sign it is not accomplished
yet the death of the spirit: angels
move among us at first light
over the fields   mysterious
as April in the grey
wood of our garden trees.

Exile

Estonian ghosts of
riverbirds within the
temples of his skull, ashes
of poets, girders of school houses:
these are the tired politics
that vein his eyes

scoop a pouch under his lower
lip. In our system
his vigour has aged into
rumours of miraculous
sexual prowess, yet
the gesture of his
pasty fist is continuous with
the sag of his cardigan

and his enemies are
quiet middle-aged men, who
move in the mist of invisible
English power. He is
unhunted and unforested in the fen:
like the rest of us.

I have seen worse days turn

However, the hot grey streets are still lit
with the flash and flicker of
overnight television, so I may
throw the morning away like
dirty water out of a cup.

Why not? Outside, the rain
and humus taste of old potatoes, which
in unfastidious hands could
blow up the whole alembic.

How do you change the weather in the blood?

For Malcolm Lowry

Salt in the notch of my
    thumb. Lemon. Tequila
on my tongue. Warm and aromatic.
    Juice of your cactus god.

Yet I would not filch from your
    Saint of desperate
and dangerous courses.
    Any flu-ridden and scraggy

one of us in a fever now
    can enter through your
thrown away papers into
    some Mexico of prescience.

Not Tequila more than gregory
    powder will I honour, but that
enormity of remaining awake, inside
    the sick pain of your head

as you went on. Choosing words to hold the red
    light of the heat had cracked through your
adobe skull. So they still should carry.
    The last flow of. Your fear-sodden blood.

Marriage

Is there ever a new beginning when every
word has its ten years' weight, can there be
what you call conversation between us?
Relentless you are as you push me
to dance and I lurch away from you
weeping, and yet can we bear to lie
silent under the ice together like
fish in a long winter?

A letter now from York is a reminder of
windless Rievaulx, the hillside moving through
limestone arches, in the ear's liquid the
whir of dove notes: we were a fellowship of three
strangers walking in northern brightness, our
searches peaceful, in our silence the
resonance of stones only, any celibate
could look for such retreat, for me
it was a luxury to be insisted on
in the sight of those grass-overgrown dormitories

We have taken our shape from the
damage we do one another, gently as
bodies moving together at night, we amend
our gestures, softly we hold our places:
in the alien school morning in the
small stones of your eyes I know how
you want to be rid of us, you were
never a family man, your virtue is
lost, even alikeness deceived us
love, our spirits sprawl together
and both at last are distorted

and yet we go toward birthdays and other
marks   not wryly   not thriftily
waiting, for where shall we find it, a
joyous, a various world? in fury
we share, which keeps us, without
resignation: tender whenever we touch   what
else we share   this flesh   we
bring together   it hurts to
think of dying as we lie close

Waiting

The house is sick. When I come down
at night to the broken kitchen, the open wall, and find
a grey-haired and courteous old
cat asleep in a design of gypsum on the ground:
I sense between iron girders and old
gas-pipes how many more ill-lit creatures of a damp
garden are waiting. Under the provisional blossom
of a plum tree they threaten a long siege
whispering: they shall eat sorrow
which is the flesh of the rat, the
dead limb in the locked room.
And I can hardly remember the dream of sunlight and
hot sweet wall-flowers that led us to break through
to the almost forgotten lord of the dark outside
whose spectres are part of his word, and whose promise of
home always demands the willingness to move on: who
forces me to acknowledge his ancient sign.

Out of touch

Now west down George Street a
star red as charred coal
blocks the line of the traffic

so that all the waiting cars
are made into shadows and
the street walls are red stained

and into that March sun   you
move off lost   another shadow
against the stones of

a spectral city: love
don't be lonely   don't let us
always be leaving singly on

some bleak journey   wait for me:
this   deliberate world   is
rapidly losing its edge.

Memory

How readily now do I forgive you
Mother your hot eyes filling
behind glass your lips pursed
at my doings. Like a nun
you smiled towards my
Father in the hospital;
when you were ill he lay on the
floor howling and had to be doped

and 4 months later he had you typing
the office mail after the dishes
again, and dourly you sat there
spelling and phrasing for him
in that bullied quiet of yours: as
though vexed by your own endurance

A quiet war in Leicester

the shelter, the old washhouse
water limed the walls
we only entered once or twice
cold as a cellar we
shivered in the stare
of a bare electric light

and nothing happened:
after the war
ants got in the sandbags
builders came

and yet at night
erotic with the
might-be of disaster
I was carried into
dreaming with delight

Our vegetable love shall grow

Shaking in white streetlight in
a cold night wind, two luminous blue fangs
push through the grass at the bus shelter:
an early crocus, drawing colour from
some hidden underfoot bulb. And now, mindless
desperate lonely waiting in a fen wind, we
barely move in our great coats, while that
blue piece of adventuring
takes all the electric of human light into
the beauty of its present flesh.

The Asthmatic

smiles and sings, in
   daylight, her
mouth curved upward
   with the taste of air.
She is sharp and joyful
   as a bird without memory

of black   gasp
   and gape of broken
mouth   blood
   wheezing for
harsh   air
   .face wrung into
baby grimace, crying
please, like a dying creature

morning   was it   the
   light strangling
behind trees or
   when did she
find herself in the hospital
   attached to a machine?

Even now, she uses her night spray:
and still she laughs eagerly.

Bathroom

My legs shimmer like fish
my hair floats on the water:
tonight I observe that my
skin is no longer smooth
that blue veins show
in my arms that my
breasts are smaller

and lie seeing still water
meeting a white sky
(my elbows swim for me)
waiting for those
queer trails of thought
that move toward sleep

to where
the unforgiven words are
stored in circuits
of cells that hold
whatever shape there is
of the lost days

For Brighton, old bawd

Streets smelling of vinegar, fronted with junk
and monstrous sweet shops, here the sea slopes up as
bland as a green hill. And the air is a wash of

salt and brightness. This town has so transfigured
the silt of what lay in our mouths that
now we can lie happily awake together as

the first milk bottles go down on the
steps and the early lorries change gear
at the lights beneath us.

Though what is good in this city is frivolous
as the green tits on Mrs. Fitzherbert's
pleasure palace, it retains the force

which is the magic of all bawdy: fit
forgiveness / that true measure / for every
shape of body and each mistaken piece of behaviour

Offering: for Marina Tsvetayeva

Through yellow fingers smoke rises about you
now we enter your transfigured life
what were those recoveries
of hope you kept to
starved ferocious ill
poet rough-clothed and cold-fingered
pushed more than loss of
lovers or even a dead child over
the edge of blackness in middle age.
When you went back to Russia   to
Efron your gentle husband   a
murderer   soon murdered   was it
in loneliness   the ear and
tongue of a language you looked for?
As misery closed in, with a last
hatred   had you
abandoned that strange trust
even when you hung yourself coldly like
an unwanted dog?   O black icon.

Lines outward

Tell me your gods / to
what magnetic darkness
you are drawn
out of your skin
forbidden what is
it beckons or
do we look for in
the yard at 4 a.m. the
rain in the white lilac?
At these limits the
birds clattering the
steam rises from old
timbers, can we
(the planet turns)
in whose name enter it,
the lyric daze?

Fishing

In leaf dust, and tarred wood
the chestnut, radiant as a moving tiger
the willow falling like water spilt
yellow-green in the river: my son
sits rocking eagerly, his
arms holding his knees as I
watch the bob of his float, the changes

of moving water, moving lips and his
bright eye. He is watching for
a single gudgeon to fly up
out of the silver mud, but when
he turns, smiling

in the delicate line of his
neck I sense uncertainly how
fierce a passion he
is holding back in
his still silence.

The Poem of the End

Translated from the Russian of Marina Tsvetayeva

1

A single post, a point of rusting
   tin in the sky
marks the fated place we
   move to, he and I

on time   as death is
   prompt   strangely
too smooth the gesture of
   his hat to me

menace at the edges of his
   eyes   his mouth tight
shut   strangely too low is the
   bow he makes tonight

on time?   that false note in
   his voice, what
is it the brain alerts to and the
   heart drops at?

under that evil sky, that sign of
   tin and rust.
Six o'clock. There he is waiting
   by the post.

Now we kiss soundlessly, his
   lips stiff as
hands are given to queens, or
   dead people thus

round us the shoving elbows of
    ordinary bustle
and strangely irksome rises the
    screech of a whistle

howls like a dog screaming
    angrier, longer: what
a nightmare strangeness life is
    at death point

and that nightmare reached my waist
    only last night
and now reaches the stars, it has
    grown to its true height

crying silently love love until
    -Has it gone
six, shall we go to the cinema?
    I shout it! home!

    6

I didn't want this, not
    this (but listen, quietly,
to want is what bodies do
    and now we are ghosts only).

And yet I   didn't say it
    though the time of the train is set
and the sorrowful honour of leaving
    is a cup given to women

or perhaps in madness I
    misheard you   polite liar:
is this the bouquet that you give your
    love, this blood-stained honour?

Is it? Sound follows
    sound clearly: was it goodbye
you said? (as sweetly casual
    as a handkerchief dropped without

thought) in this battle
    you are Caesar (What an
insolent thrust, to put the
    weapon of defeat, into my hand

like a trophy). It continues. To
    sound in my ears. As I bow.
-Do you always pretend
    to be forestalled in breaking?

Don't deny this, it
    is a vengeance of Lovelace
a gesture that does you credit
    while it lifts the flesh

from my bones. Laughter   the laugh of
    death. Moving. Without desire.
That is for others now
    we are shadows to one another.

Hammer the last nail in
    screw up the lead coffin.
-And now a last request.
    -Of course. Then say nothing

about us   to those who will
    come after me. (The sick
on their stretchers talk of spring.)
    -May I ask the same thing?

-Perhaps I should give you a ring?
  -No. Your look is no longer open.
The stamp left on your heart
  would be the ring on your hand.

      So now   without any scenes
        I must swallow, silently, furtively.
      -A book then? No, you give those
        to everyone, don't even write them

      books . . . .

So now   must be no
so now   must be no
must be no crying

In wandering tribes of
fishermen brothers
drink without crying

dance without crying
their blood is hot, they
pay without crying

pearls in a glass
melt, as they run their
world   without crying

      Now I am going and this
      Harlequin gives his
      Pierrette a bone like
      a piece of contempt

      He throws her the honour
      of ending, the curtain, the last
      word when one inch of lead in
      the breast would be hotter and better.

Cleaner. My   teeth
press my lips. I can
stop myself crying

pressing the sharpness
into the softest
so / without crying

so tribes of nomads
die without crying
burn without crying

So tribes of fishermen
in ash and song can
hide their dead man.

   8

Last bridge   I won't
give up or take out my hand
this is the last bridge
the last bridging between

water   and firm land:
and I am saving these
coins for death
for Charon, the price of Lethe

this   shadow money
from my dark hand I press
soundlessly into
the shadowy darkness of his

shadow money it is
no gleam and tinkle in it
coins for shadows:
the dead have enough poppies

This bridge

[41]

Lovers for the most
part are without hope: passion
also is just
a bridge, a means of connection

It's warm: to nestle
close at your ribs, to move in
a visionary pause
towards nothing, beside nothing

no   arms no   legs
now, only the bone of my
side is alive where
it presses directly against you

life in that side
only, ear and echo is it: there
I stick like white to
egg yolk, or an eskimo to his fur

adhesive, pressing
joined to you: Siamese
twins are no nearer.
The woman you call mother

when she forgot
all things in motionless triumph
only to carry you:
she did not hold you closer.

Understand: we have
grown into one as we slept and
now I can't jump
because I can't let go your hand

and I won't be torn off
as I press close to you: this
bridge is no husband
but a lover: a just slipping past

our support: for the
river is fed with bodies!
I bite in like a tick
you must tear out my roots to be rid of me

like ivy   like a tick
inhuman   godless
to throw me away like a thing, when there is

no thing I ever prized
in this empty world of things.
Say this is only dream,
night still and afterwards morning

an express   to Rome?
Granada? I won't know myself
as I push off
the Himalayas of bedclothes.

But this dark is deep:
now I warm you with my blood, listen
to this flesh.
It is far truer than poems.

If you are warm, who
will you go to tomorrow for that?
This is delirium,
please say this bridge cannot

end

    as it ends.

Poems for Blok

Translated from the Russian of Marina Tsvetayeva

Your name is a   bird in my hand
a piece of   ice on the tongue
one single movement of the lips.
Your name is: five signs,
a ball caught in flight, a
silver bell in the mouth

a stone, cast in a quiet pool
makes the splash of your name, and
the sound is in the clatter of
night hooves, loud as a thunderclap
or it speaks straight into my forehead,
shrill as the click of a cocked gun.

Your name   how impossible, it
is a kiss in the eyes on
motionless eyelashes, chill and sweet.
Your name is a kiss of snow,
a gulp of icy spring water, blue
as a dove. About your name is: sleep.

Insomnia

Translated from the Russian of Marina Tsvetayeva

In my enormous city it is   night,
as from my sleeping house I go   out,
and people think perhaps I'm a daughter or wife
but in my mind is one thought only   night.

The July wind now sweeps a way for   me,
From somewhere, some window, music though   faint.
The wind can blow until the dawn   today,
in through the fine walls of the breast rib-cage.

Black poplars, windows, filled with   light.
Music from high buildings, in my hand a flower.
Look at my steps   following   nobody
Look at my shadow, nothing's here of me.

The lights   are like threads of golden beads
in my mouth is the taste of the night   leaf.
Liberate me from the bonds of   day,
my friends, understand: I'm nothing but your dream.

Who sleeps at night? No one is sleeping.
   In the cradle a child is screaming.
An old man sits over his death, and anyone
   young enough talks to his love, breathes
into her lips, looks into her eyes.

Once asleep   who knows if we'll wake again?
We have time, we have time, we have time to sleep!
From house to house the sharp-eyed
   watchman goes with his pink lantern
and over the pillow scatters the rattle
   of his loud clapper, rumbling.

Don't sleep! Be firm! Listen, the alternative
is   everlasting sleep. Your   everlasting house!

Sybil

The present holder of the papers sits
behind broken glass in the derelict warehouse
androgynous, black-skulled, and ricket-boned
grimacing to deride her visitors,

skinny, tobacco-stained, alert, she has
bartered her memories of
bark smells, wild
almonds and water plants to
taste the sour air of neglected cities.

Trembling with adrenalin of
indignation, like euphoria, she
licks her lips at the modern
crystal set in the wall. Look,

it is all happening again.
We can watch together
how terror smiles through the screen
like a handsome peasant with his violin.

She sits and nods and waits for
the latest obsequies, with
a squint eye and a slant hand, she
writes: beware this generation's prophecies.

The Medium

My answer would have to be music
which is always deniable, since in my
silence, which you question, is only a landscape

of water, old trees and a few irresolute
birds. The weather is also inconstant.
Sometimes the light is golden, the leaves unseasonable.

And sometimes the ice is red, and the moon
hangs over it, peeled, like a chinese fruit.
I am sorry not to be more articulate.

When I try, the words turn ugly as rats and
disorder everything, I cannot be quiet,
I want so much to be quiet and loving

If only you wanted that. My sharpest thoughts
wait like assassins always in the dry wheat. They
chat and grin. Perhaps you should talk to them?

Night thoughts

Uncurtained, my long room floats on
    darkness, moored in rain,
my shelves of orange skillets
    lie out in the black grass.
Tonight I can already taste
    the wet soil of their ghosts.
And my spirit looks through the glass:
    I cannot hold on for ever.

No tenure, in garden trees, I
    hang like a leaf, and stare
at cartilaginous shapes
    my shadow their visitor.
And words cannot brazen it out.
    Nothing can hold for ever.

'The only good life is lived without miracles'

(N. Mandelstam)

Under hot white skies, if we could,
in this city of bridges and pink stone live gratefully
here is a lacework of wooden ghosts from New Guinea
Etruscan jewels, beetles with scales of blue mineral.

Bad news follows us, however. I wonder if
anyone walks sanely in middle age. Isn't there
always some desperation for the taste of one last
miraculous fruit, that has to be pulled from the air?

Green

In the resonance of that
lizard colour, mottled like stone from
Eilat, with blue fruit and patches
of mud in it: my thoughts scatter

over Europe where there is water
and sunlight in collision, and green is
the flesh of Holbein's coffined Christ, and
also the liturgical colour of heaven.

In England: green is innocent as grass.

Nachtfest

Water black water at night the Rhine and
in small boats lanterns like
coloured souls solemnly passing

into darkness, into circles of silver, into
black quick currents of water hidden as
the trees that rise over us steeply

up to the pink stone of the Munster, floating in
floodlight, Erasmus lies there lost, the leaves of
green and gold tile are shining,

fountains of white fire pour down the living
cliffs of pine, over drinking Baselers, a
mist of flies

gathers around the bulbs of the
bandstand. Now on a darkened raft held by ropes invisibly
in the centre of the river

men prepare the festival rockets, when
in spasms of red and green those sticks shoot
into the sky, their

light draws our breath upwards, we are gone
over the low moon after them into a
black imagination of depth more final than water.

The Sources

And how to praise them? Through the bad teeth of Europe
                                                    we had
    tasted the breath of the Bruges canals, between old
houses, water and lichen ate into us;
    and we had slept by the waters of Köln, where
detergent fluff rises every morning from the river at
                                                    sunlight.

Yet the sources are not gentle. Through the wet brown
                                                    caves of
    Trümmelbach, there is a ceaseless rush of water, one
                                                    solid
thrust through the mountain, listen, in that sound is the
                                                    whole
    force of the planet. Yes, delicate under the
trees, quietly over stones to rock pools, shining
    between grass, sometimes in a
long slow fall of fine spray vanishing or in rain
    a smell of the soil in a night of blue lightning.
The true beauty of fall is fierce. Drenched and shaking
    what frail homage to so brutal a purity?

At the edge

1

In your delirium your eyelids were
    raisin brown, and your beard like wet straw.
We were washed in salt on the same pillow together
    and we watched the walls change level gently as water.

But now there are white drops at the window
    this morning, in grey light, your fever gone,
do you even remember the dance of words that
    slipped between us like fish? My sober love.

2

Behind your darkness and
marooned again: I know that
island, sisters, where you wait to
offer your magenta crenellations
to some explorer, unafraid of the moon.

Yet I would bless you with no
causewayside, no mainland even,
but only more silence for you to turn in
so you receive at last whatever
light your creole petals need to open.

3

Into sleet over
stones and shells
on a visit to Winchelsea
to that lake of wet sand and sky where
the red water runs
salt from
sun into sea,

we laughed
crunching over
snow pouches to leap
at the planet's periphery
but our cries
died about us:

we were
black points upon
too inhuman a canvas
and were dwindling fast.
It was not just the Ural wind
drove us
inland for shelter.

A September friend

Through your erotic landscape lit with tallow flares
grotesque and valiant lady of red eyes
you move as slowly as a boat dragged overland:
while lamed and sleepless creatures hop
after you, or fall out of your skirt.

With lonely stamina you spin the
necessary thread to hide your movements.
Why should we try to judge
your true direction? Fluently
as the grass darkens and the rain begins to
fall through sulphurous trees like strings of glass

iron wheels will roll us all underground.
Their growl is in my ears, even as I
now call up the last of your shifting images
with sadness: for you bear yourself bravely.

The Celebrants

1

   Remember Melusine
morose spectre, whose own superstition once
   made a serpent of her: she was
betwitched   into a myth   by chance
   out of her housekeeping because
she was credulous, and so wandered in
   bands of the spell-bound until
she fell into encephalitic trance. And still
   to her believing company she slithered
in green skin to the last day of her life.

2

Might be anyone's cracked daughter
sozzled, or skewed of vision, lonely,
in winter months invoking mutinous powers

that pour like mercury out of the moon
into the waiting mind with its own glass-lined
pumice craters and stains of orange oxide,

always the occult temptation, the erotic
world-flicker, shining in wet streets
like coal with streaks of mica, for

the demons rise at the first oblique
longing, they rise up nocturnal and cruel, and
the neophyte becomes their stammering mouth,

breaks into joy without drugs
dangerous, cannibal, frenetic with
forbidden knowledge, in deaf violence.

Bitten with toxic spiders, women
dance themselves into exhaustion knowing
the spirits that they bear are hostile

and yet are proud to be a hostage to them,
as if their hallucinations could be
a last weapon against humiliation:

Listen to their song: as
servants of the tribe they now
enter the crisis of their terror

willing to free us from the same service,
but their song draws us after them and
some will follow   into their own unreason.

3

Trees, under wet trees, I am beckoned down to a river
that runs into land through a sink of sedge and rushes,
white trench gas, between roots galled with witches fungus
cut stumps, where bodies of bald dogs stir at the crunch of
                                                         my feet.

The mud and black leaves are frozen these last hours of the
year, I follow this sloping path downwards, like a lost
                                                   sleeper, in
fear of finding the faces, and hearing the voices, of those
who came this way   by the black stub alder   and under

in frost against spindle shrubs, or wych Elm in tangles of
twigs, and who swim in the smoke on the stream and
                                                    beneath
the rotting bridge, and float head-high in the dark
                                              evergreen
yews, and hang waiting in that poisonous foliage.

Through hoots of long-eared owl, gunshot, and cries of
mallard across the marsh, what I fear is to hear their voices;
those obdurate spirits, haunted and harassed, who once
came down this route and laid waste their energies here

to become mares of god, crying, and singing epiphanies.
They offered their eyes and their entrails for the forest
spirits to fill them like swallow-tailed kites:
they bartered their lives and the air tastes of their
                                                  drowning.

      4

In the last hour of the magus, then as now, marauding
      students went about selling horoscopes from
Lisbon to Lithuania, diseases also wandered freely
      as any demons: plague, syphilis, cholera.

The kitchens of sober doctors glittered with
      sulphur, they cast urine, read
propitious constellations and applied their
      ostrich feathers, viper fat, mummy powder.

In miniver fur, bald, with a
      sword in his pommel, tricky as any sorcerer,
Paracelsus often cured his patients,
      for which the burghers hounded him as Faustus,

Because he treated the sword instead of the wound
    believing in the natural magic of
healing in the flesh, with herbs and metals
    he challenged the dominion of the stars.

For such heresy he was nearly hanged at
    Salzburg, driven out of Poland, and of
Prussia, and at the last, without any follower
    he left Switzerland

without shoes or bag or even a stick
    in token that his realm was
not of this world, and yet doubting
    what entrance he could have to any other.

    5

And this knowledge enters even
    between the bodies of lovers, though
we share each other's vigil: that our arms

hold water only, salt as the sea
    we come from, a spongework of
acid chains, our innermost landscape

an arcane pulp of flexible
    chemistry; sinus, tubes,
follicles, cells that wander

from red marrow in the crevices
    of our long bones across
membranes, blood-stream, thymus,

and lymph nodes   to defend
    our separate skin-bound
unit of internal territory.

Give me your astrolabe and now tell me
    what doing or refusing kills
or how we will our bodies treachery.

6

The red giant Antares is in Scorpio;
    in fen fields a radio dish listens.
Who will give us a horoscope for the planet?
    On December 3 which is the Day of the Emigrant,

for those who come of the ancient tribe of Habiru
    nomads, wilderness people, having no
house of their own, or magicians; my desert
    grandmother laughed at the time to come.

Since then her daughters have seen Babylon
    Persepolis, Delphi, settled in Toledo
risen, and been flung over
    the north coast of Africa as Marranos.

From Clermont, the hill of the first Crusade
    we learnt things could be good only so long.
Our poets wrote that halls in heaven opened
    only to the voice of song, but their

boldest praise was always for
    the holy stamina of body and spirit as one
which is the only sacrament will stand to
    cold, fatigue, waiting, and starvation.

7

Lonely as a hangman through
    sweet mustard streets, at seventy
being sad and wily and austere

Buonarotti worked in fear
    for his soul, living
in prudence and squalor.

For our wood dries out,
    we shall not be
green again. In all

the bull-strong beauties of
    his torso he let in
the pressure of death,

he made it known, and
    in his dead Christ also
the full weight of strength

in a dead man. Yet where
    is the protection of
the broken body put under the ground?

8

Fear the millennial cities
    jasper-lit, descending
with oil and wine and corn
    from ancient prophecies,

where men with lidless eyes
    through centuries will slither
in holy crystal streets
    on the blood of massacre.

Their secret flagellant rites
    and luminous scars declare
a godhead and release
    for any follower,

but every incarnation, from
    Schmidt of Thuringia, to
the lost of our Los Angeles
    reveals itself in murder.

And only the bitch leader
    of a Jenghis pack can show
a spite   as human   as adepts
    of those who call Messiah.

                9

Today the air is cold and bitter as kale
    the sky porcelain, the sun bleached
to white metal: I am alight with ions

awake   alert   under
    that ancient primal blue, which is
the serene accident of our atmosphere;

tethered by winter gold in
    the hair of these
bare willows on my own green waterside.

Here birds and poets may
    sing for their time
without intrusion from

either priest or physician;
    for the Lord relents; he is
faithful. In his silence.

Having no sound or name
    he cannot be conjured.
All his greatness is in this:

to free us from the
    black drama
of the magician.

By the Cam

Tonight I think this landscape could
   easily swallow me: I'm smothering
in marshland, wet leaves, brown
   creepers, puddled in
rain and mud, one little gulp and

I'll be gone without a splutter:
   into night, flood, November, rot and
river-scud. Scoopwheeled for drainage.
   And by winter, the fen will be brittle and
pure again, an odd, tough, red leaf frozen
   out of its year into the ice of the gutter.

Patience

In water nothing is mean. The fugitive
enters the river, she is washed free;
her thoughts unravel like weeds of
green silk: she moves downstream
as easily as any cold-water creature

can swim between furred stones, brown
fronds, boots and tins the river holds equally.
The trees hiss overhead. She feels their shadows.
She imagines herself clean as a fish,
evasive, solitary, dumb. Her prayer:
to make peace with her own monstrous nature.

Some Unease and Angels

Even in May now with so many yellows:
    falling burberry, broom, birds with
feathers like wild tobacco, hot sun;
    some unease disturbed me, some

music of notes pitched too high even for
    dogs or prisoners, or the sick, as if there
were messengers asleep in the grass like pollen
    waiting to rise up in sudden flower

angels or darker sentinels, closing in on us
    all year, unkillable presences, they are
waiting to shrivel us even now, if we dare to
lift their hoods and confront them without fear.

Coastline

This is the landscape of the Cambrian age:
   shale, blue quartz, planes of slate streaked with
iron and lead; soapstone, spars of calcite;
   in these pools, fish are the colour of sand,
velvet crabs like weeds, prawns transparent as water.

This shore was here before man. Every tide
   the sea returns, and floats the bladderwrack,
The flower animals swell and close over creatures
   rolled-in, nerveless, sea-food, fixed and forgotten.

My two thin boys balance on Elvan Stone
   bent-backed, intent, crouched with their string and pins,
their wet feet white, lips salt, and skin wind-brown,
   watching with curiosity and compassion:
further out, Time and Chance are waiting to happen.

Ten poems from A City Calendar

In the landscape of cities
my blood moves to the seasons
in the brick and the tarmac
through my streets and my alleys
moving bikes and Mercedes
flash in rain and the sun,
and miraculous trees
are the guests of my garden.

From the lattice bridge this January a woman
goes in slippers over the sludge, the
snow wind parting her black hair to the skin

and as she reaches the gas-lit
passageway where music rises from
basement grids, observe: her red grin.

She is walking through an
old anger somewhere lost in
the.round of her head, and when

her lips move, the words fall
like pieces of rainy sky
or stones of tourmaline.

She is a winter troll. Miriam
wild sister dance for us
our words are transparent stones

and here we are at
the northern edge of the wilderness.

In the true weather of their art
these silver streets bustle, skin lit towers:
we break some magic barrier into
the daylight of the Duc de Berry's golden hours
and now in a supernatural city what is
possible changes as the
tones of tired voices lift
in the mild air
and like a tree
that might find loose birds in its
leafless hair, I am
open to surprises of the season

Now it is blue April again, blue as
rosemary, and birdsong begins at six;
black twigs open.
There are dark green stars on the clematis,
and every day is a day won from darkness:
from the soil, clay soil, and the earth's dominion.
The evening light gathers, the outlines thicken
where there was tracery now
there is mass and solidity,
blunt figures moving away through the glass.
The forsythia is a deranged yellow
holding the last of the sun
April again, evening and birdsong.
Listen
you can hear the year beginning,

and people singing again in birds plume and
knife pleats.
And the shop windows pretend Summer's begun.

Free day   unmarked   open
   as though in the ochre of
river light for a breath
   even the links between the
minutes have broken

sunless in August, white
   sky, silence, skipper
butterflies; a pause

now even the most
   prudent must become as
innocent as Gimpel, mutely
   welcoming the street liar
into the room with tea, bread
   music, in quiet homage
to: discontinuity.

In lovely rain now
this two weeks' tyranny of
sun is past and the trees

are dark   the air has
shed the dry pollens.
Now the garden follows me into

the house gently and every membrane
welcomes the soft presence.
The solar blast was a

dish of silence over me:
now I look for stars or blonde
lions in the wet undergrowth.

Once level with the sycamore in
    black wood of branch and bough, I could
ride out a leafless October
    like a spectral bird: not now.

Your mark is on my wrist:
    you are there in the taste of
leaf dust and rustle of
    old paper across the park.

I took your sign because
    I wanted to carry your
one muttered offer of sanctuary
    somewhere about me like a talisman

and now it brings the lemon scent
    of love into the daily and
sporadic features of default,
    defeat. And yet I understand

the timeless darkness that
    threatens, and how soon I could
feel caught again in lost hope like
    a frog in a child's hand.

What am I doing in this chill
    city, this cold countryside,

with a bunch of fresh coriander in my basket?
    as if I didn't know these streets
will taste of mushroom and woodsmoke, fenland Autumn

always, everyone enjoys red leaves and rain, and
    nobody flinches here, not even
when, riding towards us with a bonnet hiding
    his eyes and face
oblong by oblong day the New Year approaches.

Tonight, a November fever, white
eyes of light that stare and
burn in lunatic waters. Black
city: mirror of incoherence
here in the odors of oil cloth and the
hot soap breath of the coin laundries
is the wilderness we look for. And
though we change direction again
again these ruinous weeks, my
spirit reels with it, yet for
this moment penniless not caring
dazed   a piece of paper   rain-blown:
in what fierce exultation the
street sings in me.

I can only give you   my December city
    this sodium-lit terrace and cold rain
while night flows overhead, and black trees bend
    in the flow. The birds sit heavily alone like leather sails.

If we hold together now   the year is ending
    the air will soon be warm and yellow as milk, and
even the copper husks in the garden will be green again:
    will it be in time for us, my love, in time for us?

Dad

Your old hat hurts me, and those black
    fat raisins you liked to press into
my palm from your soft heavy hand:
    I see you staggering back up the path
with sacks of potatoes from some local farm,
    fresh eggs, flowers. Every day I grieve

for your great heart broken and you gone.
    You loved to watch the trees. This year
you did not see their Spring.
    The sky was freezing over the fen
as on that somewhere secretly appointed day
    you beached: cold, white-faced, shivering.

What happened, old bull, my loyal
    hoarse-voiced warrior? The hammer
blow that stopped you in your track
    and brought you to a hospital monitor
could not destroy your courage
    to the end you were
uncowed and unconcerned with pleasing anyone.

I think of you now as once again safely
    at my mother's side, the earth as
chosen as a bed, and feel most sorrow for
    all that was gentle in
my childhood buried there
    already forfeit, now forever lost.

June

Dried up old cactus
   yellowing in several limbs
sitting on my kitchen window
   I'd given you up for dead
but you've done it again overnight
   with a tasselled trumpet flower
and a monstrous blare of red!
   So it's June, June again, hot sun
birdsong and dry air;
   we remember the desert
and the cities where grass is rare.
   Here by the willow-green river
we lie awake in the terrace
   because it's June, June again;
nobody wants to sleep
   when we can rise through the beech trees
unknown and unpoliced
   unprotected veterans
abandoning our chores
   to sail out this month in nightgowns
as red and bold as yours;
   because it's June, June again.
Morning will bring birdsong
   but we've learnt on our bodies
how each Summer day is won
   from soil, the old clay soil
and that long, cold kingdom.

Watersmeet

There are spores at work in the stone here, corded
   roots of dead trees holding back shale and wedged
rocks: the green foliage of the hillside conceals
   a perilous truce between plant and mineral powers

and wet-foot from the cold Lyn we climbed up
   from shining grit into fibrous barks, tall ferns
quartz in the soil, and everywhere plant flesh
   and rich ores had eaten into each other, so that

peat, rain, green leaves and August fused
   even the two of us together; we took
a new balance from the two defenceless
   kingdoms bonded in hidden warfare underfoot.

Homage to Marina Tsvetayeva
by three Russian poets

House in Meudon

Margarita Aliger

Grey and dingy house in Meudon,
dull and grey old house in Meudon,
flat as board   four storeys high
uncoloured brick, unlit, unchosen
there by someone else's garage, like
a burnt-out candle, dripping wax:
there it was you lived, Marina.

Grey and dingy house in Meudon.
Nothing grows on that verandah.
There's no smile behind the window,
just a dead house, stiff with cold, with
no dogs, no cats and alone
deserted like a bivouac.

How long since the Russian language
was used there? To cry or laugh or
hide your misery from children,
suffer in,   or breathe, or be
written in notebooks until morning.
Now this upright narrow house
has fallen into a French silence
with its gates closed at the bend.
It conjures up by day and night
all your memories in my heart.

From now on, to move or not, will
alter nothing. Magic cannot
change the bends that wait for you
hollows ahead, and more mirages —
houses by other people's garages.

Now I have it on my palm,
in my own hand: the dingy house.
Look, how bare it is, how lonely,
always facing down the road
three hundred metres. To the station.

—I must pack my bundle now.
—What's the hurry? Off to Paris?
What's the fever, what's the panic?
You've seen Berlin once already.
Do you want to go to Prague?
—No. I'd rather die. I'll go to
no more foreign cities. Ever.

I must go back to   Trekhprudny,
to Granatny, Plyushikha, the Arbat. . . .
Yes, let's be going. Soon, as soon
as can be. Fast. At a run.
Still the dingy house in Meudon —
Stubbornly, it's black stare follows.
While you find your last dark river
Kama, rocks, insects, and that
small town that reaches down the hill.

To the Kama, then, from Meudon.
To be without a home or foothold.

Not to prison. Not to freedom.
With a great stone in your throat.
Two years. No address. No shelter.
Without word. Without a word.
Without daughter. Without husband.
Only horror, hard frost, sirens,
and the war shriek overhead.

Still your son was with you, in that
wooden hut above the river.
Who was guilty then? Of what?
In that dark house, on that rough road.

All around you, Russia, Russia
danced in golden rings barefoot
in the small woods
                    on the steep banks,

Russia who had brought you up
a daughter once — then let you go.
So, did you displease her? How?
Because you went away from home
and lost yourself in foreign lands?
That she forgave you long ago.
Russia had no time, not then,
to understand you, all her women
wept in all the villages,
wagons always on the move
steppes on fire, and all her people
running away. How could she then
remember you? Or bother with you?
There you were. Behind the fence.
Yelabuga. The edge of war.

For no fault of yours forgotten.
Mother Russia. Mother Rus'.
This cold. Bleak. I am afraid.

What comes next Lord? Every August
is the end of Summer. So
what happens? Every year
rains come and the hardest clay

erodes, and crumbles. Winter comes.
Marina. How will you live through it?
The Kama will not move. No way
to cross. By foot or horse. No path
Or road. Only the snow. Blizzard.
No friend. Not even an enemy.
Only snow and snow and snow
like your landlady's featherbed!
You won't be able to leave the yard.
Marina. How will you live through it?
Even you can't handle this.
You've gone too far.
—Yes. This is it.
                        And your last trick?
                              A hempen rope.

Poem

Yevgeny Yevtushenko

Do you think of her, geranium Yelabuga?
　　That woman of the cities long ago
who smoked like other people cry, smoked
　　all the time, your harsh, home-grown tobacco.

This is where, dead-tired, she had to go
　　begging for linen to wash. So now
let me stand here, too, Marina;
　　for a moment let me share your place.

An old woman, worn out with opening her
　　wooden gate, said: I don't know why they
keep on coming; at my age it's torture.
　　Well, I'd sell this house but who would buy it?

Yes, I remember the woman. Strict. I knew
　　washing linen wasn't her job. She
never did learn how to roll her own fags, either
　　so I had to do it for her. Not that rope though!

And yet that wretched hemp was
　　kind to her; for the last time
she had the chance to wet her parched
　　lips again with the frozen Kama.

But look at it — a nail! Not a hook. Clumsy.
　　Used for the yokes of horses, too low to
reach for, still less hang from:
　　it would have been as easy for her to choke!

And then that old woman, who had lived right
    through the famine, spoke to me with deference.
'And how can I get *rid* of this nail now?' she asked,
    touching it. 'Do you know what I should do?

Please, listen, be kind, and tell me one thing.
    How was it she came to kill herself?
You seem to have some kind of education, so
    perhaps you understand, and can help me.'

'Granny, this small room fills me with fear. All
    I really want is to fall on your shoulder and
cry with you. Remember: there is only
    murder in this world. Suicide has no existence here.'

I Swear

Bella Akhmadulina

    by that summer snapshot taken
on someone else's porch, skewed to one
side, that looks so like a gibbet, and
points a way out of the house not into it;
where you are wearing some violent sateen dress that
cramps the muscles of your throat like armour;
and are simply sitting there, with the endurance of a
tired horse after the labour of
singing out to the end all your grief and hunger.
I swear: by the photo, and your delicate pointed
elbows, which are as child-like as the smile of surprise
that death uses to lure children to itself and leaves
as a mark upon their faces for evidence.
I swear: by the painful burden of remembering
how I gulped your airless grief from the
breathless rush of your lines, and had to
keep clearing my throat until it bled.
Yes, by your own presence, which I have stolen,
burgled, taken for myself, as if forgetting that
you belong to God, who cannot get enough of you;
and by that starved emaciation which
killed you at the end with its rat tooth.
I swear: by the blessed Motherland herself, even if
she grossly abandoned you like an orphan;
and your beloved African, that great genius of
kindness, whose own end was unkind, now
as a statue watching over small children.

By those children! And the Tversky Boulevard!
And your own sad rest in Paradise, where
there is neither trade nor torment for you!
I swear: to kill that Yelabuga, your
Yelabuga, so that our grandchildren
can sleep soundly. Old women may still frighten
them at nights, not knowing the power of her
'Sleep little child, quietly, quietly, for
blind Yelabuga is coming to catch you.'
And with all her tangle of legs truly she will
hasten towards me crawling with horrible speed.
But I shall bring my boot down on her
tentacles without saying any more, and
put my weight on my heel, and my toe-cap into
the back of her neck, and keep it there.
Then the green juice of her young will burn
the soles of my feet with their poison, but I'll
hurl the egg that ripens in her tail
into the earth, that bottomless earth!
And not say a word of the porch in the photograph.
I will not speak of Marina's homeless death.
I swear it. Even while in
the dark, and in the stench of silt,
with the toads in the well about her, she
has one yellow eye fixed in my direction:
The Yelabuga
swears her own oath — to kill me!

Yelabuga was the town in which
Marina Tsvetayeva killed herself.